God loves
you so!

"*Tragically Transformed: How God Turned Struggle to Gift* is a first chapter more than a biography. Kendra Wriston's heart is so clearly open to God that I know there is more to come. The book is honest and brave. I approached it wearing two hats– one, as a friend who has seen the transformation, and two, as a pastor-counselor who daily works with people facing life's harsh realities. In both capacities, her transparency and vulnerability rang true, and made me anxious to share it with many who will draw courage for their journey from it. It's a book that will captivate women– men need to read it, too. It gives courage and guidance to all who must embrace a new normal.

– Pastor Brenda Mason Young,
Cornerstone Church

"I have always been amazed how much or how little people rely on their faith to get them through trage- dies. Having been a small part of both Kendra's joyful and dark seasons, I am amazed and inspired by her deep reli- ance upon God. Her resilience, honesty, and faith make up a powerful story that not only needs to be told but shared with others. You can't help but be changed for the better once you hear her story."

**– Jeff Hanna, Director of the Fishfactory,
Des Moines, IA**

"Filled with pain and promise, this book is a must read for anyone dealing with life's most difficult heartache. With God continually by her side, Kendra traces the steps of a journey no one wants to take. Her story is tragic, yet encouraging as she paints a vivid picture of how precious life is while strongly relaying on the gift of God's love and mercy. I was moved and inspired by her heartfelt hon- esty, grace and courage to share her story in an effort to give others the gift of hope and healing."

**– Kelly Kotch, Associate University Registrar,
Akron, OH**

"As written on their website, Psychology Today states, "Resilience is that ineffable quality that allows some peo- ple to be knocked down by life and come back stronger than ever." I can't think of a better way to describe Kendra! Having been her friend and colleague for the past 10 years, it is obvious to see that she has a definite purpose in this world to use her own life experiences and challenges as a testimony that can add value to others who her read her story."

– Elaine Barkan, Gifted Education Consultant, Stark County, Ohio

"Kendra's first few weeks of marriage came with hopes of a bright future until it was torn from her grasp by a drunk driver. The love of her life gone and fighting for her life, she found herself in the valley of weeping. Plunged into an excruciatingly painful emotional, physical and spiritual recovery, she made the courageous decision that there was more to life than her pain. No one wants to find themselves in the valley of weeping; we fear it will completely destroy us. Kendra's story is a shining beacon that says, *'Come and see with me that your valley of weeping can become a place of springs. I know, I've been there.'*"

– Annelyse DeBellis, MA, LPCC-S

TRAGICALLY
TRANSFORMED

HOW GOD
TURNED STRUGGLE
TO GIFT

KENDRA WRISTON

Follow me on Facebook: *Tragically Transformed: How God Turned Struggle to Gift*
Follow me on Instagram: *@kswtragicallytransformed*

Cover & Interior Design: D.E. West / ZAQ Designs - Dust Jacket Creative Services

Printed in the United States of America

TABLE of CONTENTS

ACKNOWLEDGEMENTS

This book would not have been completed without the unending support of my family and friends. Dad, Mom, Kasey, Troy, it has been a true blessing traveling the ups and downs of life with you. Your care, encouragement, grace, support, and unconditional love are a true blessing. We have traveled this journey together and I have been grateful for you every step.

Thank you to my friends I consider my sisters. You have loved me through my darkest and brightest days. You have prayed and cared for me; supported and encouraged me. I am grateful for our shared laughs and tears. I am undeservingly blessed to have you in my life.

I would like to extend a special thank you to my Pastor, Brenda Young, for your writing mentorship, spiritual guidance, friendship, and encouragement. Jim loved you, and I continue to love you. To my counselor, Annelyse DeBellis, you have helped me grow through the trauma and grieving process. Your support, wisdom, grace, and spiritual knowledge have helped reach a place of healing I would not otherwise have achieved. You are a treasure. There is not a day that I don't praise Jesus for the many medical professionals involved in this journey. I am literally standing here today because of you.

For my Jim, who loved me with all he had until the day he went to heaven.

INTRODUCTION

I'll never forget the moment I received a return email from a publishing company stating they would be honored to work with my book. Of course I was out with friends and cried as I read the email aloud. It was such a bittersweet moment. The obvious truth is, this isn't the story I wanted to write, nor the journey would I have chosen for the past seven years. When I married Jim on November 12, 2011, I was hoping our story would be filled with children, a dog, white-picket fences, and many years of being married to each other.

Sadly, our story did not unfold that way. I never dreamed we would be in a car accident, hit by a drunk driver. I never dreamed I would be a widow after only five weeks of marriage. I would never wish my heartbreak, loss, physical pain, rehabilitation, or struggles through grief on anyone.

As I look in the mirror today, I see a completely different person than I did seven years ago. God has done amazing work in me. He has restored and rebuilt. He has loved, healed, and comforted. God continues to transform me from the inside out. You will never hear me say I'm glad the accident happened, but I will sing all day about the good God has done since it.

Throughout this book, I granted myself permission to be the most authentic me. I work hard, play hard, love hard, grieve hard, heal hard. I'm equal parts head and heart, action and thought. Life can be funny, so go ahead and laugh at it. I make mistakes, I learn, I grow. I'm a life-long learner and a relational-introvert. Through God, I'm more than just a sad story.

Loss, of any kind, is unbearable. Grief is not for the faint of heart. Some days during the last seven years it seemed if my body didn't breathe on its own, then I would surely suffocate. I miss Jim so much and long to be with him. I rest in the comfort that he is in heaven with our Savior and I will be reunited with him someday…But today is not that day!

Grief has taught me that I'm alive, and I'm alive for a purpose. It teaches me to live better than I have before. It teaches me to love more deeply. Grief helps me intentionally choose what I participate with, look at, and hear. I'm encouraged to no longer give life's obstacles undue power—and I want to encourage you in the same way.

Significant prayer has been offered over this book. Despite concern it was too large a task for "little old me," I've truly never been so honored as to write this book. To see the world through one word at a time, watch it form sentences, then paragraphs, and pages, has been a blessing. I am thankful for you, my Reader. I pray you always know God loves you and you are not alone; that you will believe you can grow through struggle, coming out better and stronger on the other side

CHAPTER ONE

DADDY'S GIRL!

"A girl's first true love is her father."
– Marisol Santiago

Minerva held that small town, close knit community feel that one familiar with small towns might expect. The town of Minerva and my family are key to who I am. As a child I loved hearing stories told by my high school teachers who taught my parents before me. Sadly, I wasn't given permission to share any of the good ones! Apparently my father, Ken, was a little more school-oriented, and my mother, Kay, was a little more socially-oriented. High school sweethearts, they married at 21 when my dad was still in college and my mom had joined the workforce. They are a great team, even 41 years later. I am in love with the way they are in love with each other. My dad is a leader—strong, emotional, athletic, encouraging, serving, a deep thinker, wise, driven, and an amazing husband and father. He thrives as provider and protector. He retired from teaching after 36 ½ years and had served as a long term, multiple sports coach. It pleases me to have followed in my father's footsteps as a teacher—and I even coached for eight years. Dad now has a second career as a church pastor.

For many years my mother worked outside of the home in the business arena, but has spent the vast majority of her time as an amazing homemaker. She is a cancer survivor, strong, supportive, nurturing, emotional, tender-hearted, serving, organized, intelligent, and is the ultimate caregiver for all of my family. She is an amazing wife and mother. Seeing her embrace and excel in the role of a pastor's wife during this season fills me with joy. I value her profession as a homemaker, not only because of the pride she has in it and the joy she gets from it, but also because I am still hoping that more of it rubs off on me. I am naturally more like my father, but I've always been told that daughters turn into their mothers as they get older. I'm so glad I'm finding that statement to be true.

Kasey, my sister and only sibling, is 4 ½ years younger than I, is very similar to my mother in so many ways. I love her dearly. Kasey is one of the most joyful, easy going, accepting people I know. She met her husband, Troy, in high school, married him a few years later, and they still have a thriving relationship. Secretly, I nurture some resentment that she acquired all of the cooking talent in the family. I joke at her expense at times, but if you say anything out of turn about her, this big sister bear goes into attack mode.

As a family, we have lost our share of loved ones and faced our own health scares. We've had our own private, personal struggles. We have our flaws and disagreements. When one person hurts, we all hurt. When one celebrates, we all celebrate. We are better together. We may not always like, but we do always love. For all these things, we are stronger and closer. We are a family that works hard, plays hard, moves forward, enjoys all, and chooses to minimize the bad and maximize the good. And yes, we are a family of Ks!

Growing up a tom-boy in the 1980s, I had fun toys like He-Man, Star Wars, and a variety of sports equipment. Most of my limited TV time was spent cheering on the Chicago Bears, laughing at sitcoms, and wanting to be Wonder Woman…Full disclosure: I'm still half-convinced I AM her! Many days I went with my dad to two-a-day football practices, or I wrestled my sister—and anyone else who would indulge me—on the wrestling mat. I don't think my sister enjoyed that time as much as I did. I had an imaginary friend named Wilma. She and I used to play outside for hours at a time. I'm thankful that my parents believed that was creative play and never assumed I was crazy. Secretly, I've always thought the world inside my head was always larger and better than the one that played out in real life. I was involved in the church youth group and Vacation Bible School. Summers were for family time, sports, outdoors, beach vacations. Mini-brag moment: I was one of the first girls in town to play boys' fast pitch baseball. I always had this feeling the world was bigger than just me, and I had a lot to offer it. I was just a bit stubborn, a leader, driven, too smart for my own good—or at least I thought I was. I generally recharged from time spent alone. I'm sure some of the areas in my life that frustrated my parents as I was growing up were actually God instilling groundwork and strengths necessary for this journey. I credit my parents so much, not only because I appreciate the way they raised us, but also because I view parenting as the toughest of all jobs. I guess one tends to see that as they get older.

Going through school in the same district where my father taught definitely helped keep me on track. I was still ornery; I got caught from time to time. I enjoyed school and earned good grades. Some subjects demanded that I work a little harder than others, but perseverance is definitely a positive family trait. Even though I quietly desired to be popular and please all people, I wasn't and I couldn't. I played sports, sung in choir, participated in band, performed in drama, joined various clubs, and socialized with a diverse group of friends.

My family lost our house to a fire during my school years. I am thankful for the hard lessons I learned through it. It was the first time I realized that some things just couldn't be controlled or fixed. It was also the first time I experienced beauty rising from the ashes. During this time, I began to develop goals for the future. I knew early on I wanted to go to the same college as my father, and I desired to be a teacher. Rather than spending my time getting caught up in the usual drama of high school, I built my resume to get into Mount Union College, now known as the University of Mount Union, a good school near home.

I loved my Mount Union College experience and remain a grateful alumnus. I would not want to go back and do it again, but those years were filled with fun and a variety of experiences. I think experience can be a great teacher, and I learned a lot over those four years. Like in high school, I enjoyed learning, earned good grades, and worked hard. I loved being out on my own. I joined a sorority, Alpha Xi Delta, a great group of women, and eventually became president of that sorority. I played intramural sports and received a scholarship to play trumpet in the band. I worked on campus during the school year and over summer. I was still involved in multiple clubs and had a group of good friends. I started to date more and realized that I wanted someone serious with whom to share my life. My boyfriend asked me to marry him during my senior year and I said yes! Student teaching felt like a real life job that I enjoyed. I was hired to teach at Canton Local School District soon after graduating in 2001 and was excited to be planning a wedding. Things were coming together nicely. Exactly according to plan, it seemed.

…Until a few months later when I called off the wedding. It just didn't feel right, and deep down I knew I wasn't supposed to marry him. I'm pretty sure he felt the same. Even though we both had doubts, pride and anger got in the way and it ended badly. My parents welcomed me back home for a few months before renting an apartment on my own. But my doubts didn't settle. "Aren't you ready to get married and have kids yet?" I was asked that question repeatedly. The expectation seemed huge— and I had failed. The picture in my head looked so much different than the reality I was actually living. I was a bit lost and wandering for the next six years.

I loved teaching, being independent, and I had good friends; however, something was missing. I dated numerous Mr. Wrongs because it was easy and they were there, but nothing ever progressed to the next step. It was discouraging at the time. Now I see it as a blessing. I did not realize that my relationship with God was slowly deteriorating like a plant I never watered. My exterior image said things were great, but secretly my interior knew better. As an introvert, my family always said that I am able to mask how I really feel if I choose. I found it easy to take the path of comfort and convenience. Somehow I imagined if I kept walking on that path, it would eventually get me to the desired destination. I was wrong. I know now what I couldn't see then: I was making unhealthy choices to cope and navigate through life.

And then, a change was offered to me, a defining moment. A friend invited me to church with her one Sunday. I hadn't consistently attended church in a few years, but I figured it would be good social time at least. We traveled to Cornerstone Free Methodist Church in Akron, Ohio. I felt like the woman pastor was speaking directly to me—I loved it and needed it! Nearly seven years later, I am deeply connected in this church community, growing in fellowship, becoming more involved, being challenged, and growing in Christ. Eventually, this same church would be the scene of my greatest joy and share my deepest sorrow. God's hands were weaving something I could not have imagined.

Heavenly Father,
Please help us to trust that your hands are weaving something for us that we are not yet able to imagine. Thank you for instilling the groundwork in us that we will need throughout our journey.
In Jesus name I pray,
Amen

Chapter 1 Questions for Reflection:

1. Which parent do you identify with most?

2. Think about your family traits that have been passed down through generations. Identify the traits that you think have been beneficial to your life.

3. What is some groundwork God has instilled in your life in preparation for your journey? *(see Proverbs 3:5-6)*

4. Do you have a life experience when you've seen beauty rise from the ashes?

My dad and I enjoying a family trip to Myrtle Beach! My mom is taking the picture. The beach is such a special place for my family!

I was one of the first girls to play ball with the boys! Sports are such a big part of my life!

My dad was a long-time coach. My sister and I spent many days at different practices and loved it! Here we are ready to go to wrestling practice with our matching shirts!

CHAPTER TWO

HE'S the ONE!

*"We come to love not by finding
a perfect person, but by learning to see an
imperfect person perfectly."*
– Sam Keen

They say when you find the one that's perfect for you you'll know it. Whoever "they" are, I agree with them. Jim is one of my favorite people that I love to talk, hear, and think about. Oddly enough, we were set up by hairstylist friends who heard of each of our desires to meet someone. He was red-faced and embarrassed; apologizing for the deer shirt he wore on our first date to "Chili's Grill & Bar." It was his comfortable favorite and provided some funny moments during our evening together. I still have that deer shirt. It's one of many tangible memories I hold, like the pages of his photo albums, highlighted with smiling faces, family get-togethers, friends, skiing trips, fishing trips, beach vacations, restoring and racing cars, trucks, tools, and muddy faces from four-wheeling.

Jim became my rock. There was a quiet strength about him I greatly admired. He was so genuine in even the smallest of acts. Jim loved simple things, and found great contentment in them. He had a secure, solid relationship with God, first and foremost. Then loved me with all he had, and loved others.

He was the first to say "I love you." I wept with emotion hearing it. His words were few and filled with sincerity. I blushed at how often I was told how beautiful I was. He was the most handsome man I'd ever seen, a man who took care of himself physically, mentally, spiritually. He was a handy man with dreams of someday building our house. A lover of all things vehicle, he had four-wheelers, maintained his first truck (a 1989 Chevy Cameo S10), restored a 1968 Camaro, and owned an everyday driving car and truck. He seemed nocturnal, working third shift from 10:30 pm to 6:30 am at the Timken Company. Such a hard-working man. I felt I had the great honor of being the caretaker of this emotional man's tender heart. I treasure the love notes he wrote me.

Jim's independence and self-awareness were among the first things that attracted me. There's nothing sexier than a man that knows himself well enough to be over himself. We were so safe and secure together. We had each lived as singles for quite a few years on our own; as a couple, we wanted each other more than needed each other. To be wanted was our mutual deep desire, and very healthy for us. Life can be a game of dodge ball at times, but it was nice to have a teammate to tackle the game together and divert life's attacks. Trust, commitment, and loyalty were commonalities. If we were to do something it should be done to our best. Though we had different degrees of schooling, intelligence and depth were highly compatible. We were 31 and 40 years old when we met. That was a blessing. We brought with us experience and maturity gained from lessons learned earlier in life. The merging of finances was seamless because we had established jobs using our talents. While dating, we took a financial class through our church that enabled us to talk about sharing, saving, and spending money together as a couple. Those evenings we sat and dreamed about the things our money would allow us to do in our future.

Usually there's that awkward time period while dating, when you don't know where you stand, where you are going, what to call each other. But, not for us. Jim had worked at the Timken Company for years on second shift, then was laid off for about a year. Shortly after we met, he was hired back on a day shift, knowing he would eventually have to go back to second shift. A month and a half into our relationship, he said that we needed to have a conversation about his work. He shared that he had the option to go back to second shift or work the night shift. He wanted my opinion on what he should do. Trusted with this, I tried to be unnerved, supportive. Having primarily worked a teacher's schedule, I admitted both shifts were different than anything I'd known, offered that both had positive and negative attributes, but ultimately, it was his decision. As we were discussing, he said, "Kendra, I just don't think second shift is any way to start out a family. I would be missing so much!" I was stunned and assured there would be no awkward time period for us.

We were opposites in multiple ways. Isn't it funny that sometimes our differences can both frustrate and attract us to one another? We both graduated as Minerva Lions, but Jim walked across the stage in 1989, I followed in 1997. He was the baby in his family, great brother to his sister, a devoted son, uncle to his niece and nephew. He was methodical, and even-tempered. Firstborn in my family, I am driven, a bit feisty, sometimes loading unrealistic expectations on situations. Full throttle, a control freak at times, I try to do things on my own. I over-think things and I spend a lot of time inside my own head. Jim, on the other hand, had a quiet confidence, a strength that I liked telling people about. We both enjoyed the outdoors, but he could stay outside all day and night. (I am very thankful for air conditioning!) My dating card had been punched a little more than his. My close network of friends was a bit more diverse, and larger in number. I feed off involvement in areas where I'm passionate. Our families were both very loving, yet also very different. I was the one that held onto things that he'd already let go. I love the way we laughed together. I claim the title of comedian between us. He would agree. We differed in talents, skills, experiences. In all of that, we grew closer still.

Because we were older when we met, we were both set in our own ways. This caused occasional disagreements. House hunting exposed many differences. We had different pictures of what we wanted in a home. One defining certainty was we wanted a home and life together. I was the talker, and he the good listener. This surfaced a particular disagreement. We had a little back and forth conversation, me talking too much and him too little. It made sense in my head, so I told him that I was repeating myself so much because he wasn't saying anything. We found compromise is necessary. The "Goldilocks Principle" worked for us--not too much, not too little. We developed a system for Jim to let me know if I was driving a point home too much. We amicably set up another communication system for me to set time limits for his response. Our disagreements now appear so trivial in the rear view mirror.

Absolutely we were flawed human beings with our share of similarities and differences. Wholeheartedly we chose each other every minute and were allowed to be ourselves. We prayed together for each other, family, friends, people we didn't know, and circumstances where we hoped for God to show up. God was the center of our relationship. We desired such a daily, obedient relationship with Him that we did not engage in premarital sex. This was not always the decision made with my previous relationships. Truthfully, I think abstaining was more difficult for me than him, especially as we traveled to Myrtle Beach for vacation together. But growing together in Christ and the church is such an unbreakable bond. My unconditional love for Jim was like no other. I loved how he loved me. I worked to be better. He worked to be better. Together our relationship would thrive. This was the beginning of our story. We knew we had the time to enjoy, make mistakes, grow, build, serve, love, and experience. Jim was worth it. We were worth it. I was ready for it. Our love was like any hard fought sports game I've played in or coached. When the final buzzer rang, there was no loser. We just ran out of time.

Heavenly Father,

In all our flaws and imperfections, thank you for loving us perfectly. Please help us to give both ourselves and others the grace to be who we really are in you. Only you are the author of our stories. Continue to grow us and surround us with thriving relationships in our lives. May we point others to you.

In Jesus name I pray,

Amen

Chapter 2 Questions for Reflection:

1. What are some characteristics essential to your thriving relationships?
   (see Hebrews 10:24-25)

2. Describe one imperfectly perfect person in your life.

3. Read 1 Corinthians 13.

Jim and I are enjoying opening some gifts together, enjoying time with my family.

CHAPTER THREE

MR. & MRS. WRISTON

*"Classic fairy tales do not deny the existence
of heartache and sorrow, but they do
deny universal defeat."*
– Greenhaven

It's incredible the way someone comes into your life and immediately plays a starring role in your fairy tale. Jim and I were engaged on April 15, 2011 after dating for nine months. So tender-hearted, this man cried, and told me how much he loved me. He said he wanted to spend the rest of his life with me, and asked if I felt the same about him. When he pulled out this shiny, beautiful diamond, I emphatically said, "yes!" Our seven-month engagement made for some exciting celebrating, planning, and anticipation. We couldn't wait to start spending our lifetime together. I was the one warming my cold feet a few weeks before our wedding. That's a little hard to admit!

November 12, 2011 arrived; the much-anticipated wedding day. It was perfect. I'm sure everyone says that, but let me tell you, it was truly perfect for us. Everything we could have ever wanted. Jim and I had a small wedding, only close family and friends in attendance, with a dinner-only reception afterwards. My mother made Cornerstone Church beautiful—fit for a goddess. This truly would be the scene of my greatest joy! Jim melted hearts, especially mine, when he cried as my father walked me down the aisle. Truth be told, there weren't many dry eyes at our wedding. And though a big wedding dress just didn't suit this tom-boy, I could tell Jim secretly wanted a dress, so a dress he got. He made my heart stop, looking so handsome in his suit. We wanted our wedding to remain intimate, so my sister, Kasey, was my only bridesmaid; Jim's lifelong best friend was his best man. Jim's father told me that he was filled with joy as it had been 42 years since he welcomed a daughter into the family. Our pastor, gifted with eloquence and close knowledge of us from church and premarital counseling, announced us as man and wife.

We were eager to enjoy our first married night together after being pronounced as husband and wife, and we were home by 9:30pm. We left for a short honeymoon stay in Berlin, Ohio because we were planning a beach getaway in June. As I've overheard many brides explain they don't remember much from their wedding day, I am comforted that I do.

Such joy and peace came in being married in the present, but also with great hopes and dreams for our future. Life is really about enjoying the small things, and we excelled at that. I remember gratefully praying, with tears streaming down my face, thanking God for this blessing, for the man that Jim was, the team that we already were. Humbly, I was given marriage advice in my mid-20's by a gentleman married for many years. He told me, "Find the best one you can and marry him. If you love each other, serve each other, work to be better, it will be everything you've ever hoped for." I did just that. And it was.

Sunday, December 18th, 2011 started out with us sharing a morning prayer for the day, eating breakfast together. We anticipated worship and fellowship at church. Oh, how we loved church. After services, we continued the great day by traveling to my parents' house to visit with them. We left hours later with cheeks that hurt from laughter, hearts and stomachs full. We all embraced in one last hug before we left to travel home. Once in the car, as was typical, we held hands. I can still feel the warmth of his hands. We began talking about upcoming Christmas plans. Celebrating our first Christmas together as a married couple made us certain we wanted to do as much as possible to meet each other's needs, and then be with our families. Neither of us wanted to be that couple that fought or hurried through the holidays. We were sharing our desire and then all I remember is that there were bright lights coming at us from a truck plowing towards us on our side of the road.

Suddenly I knew I was no longer holding Jim's hand in the car. I woke up to bright lights, silhouettes of people that I could not distinguish.

…Blurred vision, cloudy people, rhythmic beeping sounds, tubes coming out of me. My body felt lifeless and immobile.

…Frustrated and unable to talk due to tubes down my throat.

As a few people drew closer to my face, I tried to reach to them, but quickly felt my right hand snap back. It was secured to the hospital bed. Later I was told that they fastened my hand because people's first instinct is to pull out their tubes—they know what they are talking about.

I was squirming, trying to move. I overheard a man's voice saying, "Remember this is a marathon, not a sprint." Oh, that memory. Lovingly, my mother was trying to calm

me, to no avail. I'm using the only body part that is working correctly, my right hand, to spell out the letters J-I-M
on her hand! Vigorously, I repeat this effort until finally
my dad brings his face close to mine saying six words that
forever change my life. "Jim went to be with God!"

Confusion and shock flooded over me as I stare back
at the sad, exhausted, swollen eyes staring at me. Jim had
gone to heaven instantly when we were hit by a drunk
driver who was passing another car on a hill. This had to
be a nightmare and soon I will wake up. I'm not sure what
was worse, imagining this was a horrible nightmare and
feeling that I would wake soon, or truly finding out that it
was a nightmare I was living, eyes wide open.

I spent more than two weeks in the hospital. I don't
remember asking the severity of my injuries, and no one
gave me the list either. Nearly seven years later, I weep
with overwhelming gratitude and awe of God's great
healing and provision. Now I am able to note my injuries. My left side suffered great devastation. A collapsed
lung, an 8-inch gash in my mediastinum, which allowed
other internal organs to pass through it, required lifesav-
ing measures. Immediately, I received a breathing tube,
feeding tube, chest tubes, and a central line for medications, fluids, and blood draws. Additionally, a fractured
collar bone, humerus, ribs, femur, tibia, fibula, pelvis,
ulnar styloid process; a shattered and rebuilt kneecap;

chipped vertebrae. I now resemble the Terminator. I have two titanium rods in my left leg and one in my left humerus. My mother recalls my orthopedic doctor telling her that whatever wasn't broken was splintered, bruised, or moved. Humbly, he said he put Humpty-Dumpty back together again. My abdomen and knee were just loaded with staples. Many scars of different lengths mark my body to trace an amazing only God story.

My only movement out of the hospital bed was to sit upright in a chair for some exercise. Radial nerve damage rendered my left arm and hand useless. I was originally a left-handed dominant person, however, my kindergarten teacher switched me to a right-handed dominant person. I was already thankful to her for switching dominant hands because of the ambidextrous athletic gains it provided, but I now am amazed at God's provision of what I would need for this journey. This time period of great inability made physical touch one of my top love languages because of the dedicated people who held my hand all through those weeks. One friend sat with me and *literally* held my hand at the hospital while my family attended Jim's calling hours and funeral.

Among my favorite things at Akron City Hospital were the nurses, doctors, the family and friends that braved the snowy December roads and discomfort to visit daily. I remember the awkwardness of not knowing what to talk about. While pretending to watch the New Year's Eve celebration on television, one of my favorite nurses came and silently held my hand. Neither of us had anything to say. I was numb, disbelieving, sad, lonely, questioning God why I was alive. She stayed with me in those moments. That is imprinted in me. My greatest weapon then and now was finding gratitude in the present moment.

Improvement meant I was transported to Woodlawn Rehabilitation Center for five weeks. Along with miraculous physical healing, my sense of humor returned. One day while in the hospital, a neurological specialist came in to ask mundane remedial questions to check brain function. Big praise! One of the very few parts of my body not affected by the accident was my head. As she continued to ask me questions, I respectfully replied, "I'm a genius!" The days began to lift a little with the assistance of laughter. I was quite apprehensive to leave the hospital because I didn't know what the world outside would be like for me now. The paramedic in charge of transporting me applauded the miracle I was and told me not to fear. Fear is a reasonable go-to emotion, but my emotions were absent. I was outside of that. I had nothing—nothing to lose, nothing in the present, and certainly nothing to gain.

Woodlawn was focused and intense, but slowly allowed me to begin the lengthy process of grieving. One of my first encouraging encounters was with my favorite occupational therapist. She cried with me while my sister pulled a shirt of Jim's out of the drawer for me to wear for the day. Then she said we had work to do. I had hours of painful physical and occupational therapy daily.

On top of everything else, I also had frozen joint syndrome in my lower and upper extremities because of my extended immobility. If my dad told me one more time to breathe through the pain, I felt I would give *him* something to breathe through.

At one of my lowest moments, when therapy and sorrow became too overwhelming, I told my mother that I wanted to be done. I would stay in a wheelchair. I would go home. Done. My mom pulled up her small frame to become tall and confident as she told me, "No. You are not done. God is not done!" She was correct on both accounts. The body adapts and overcomes. Before long I found myself able to function a little, using my right hand, arm, and hopping on my right leg. What was once daily normalcy—like getting dressed, using the restroom, eating—became celebrations. Woodlawn became my new home. Its routines became mine. Each day played out the same: wake up, eat, therapies, work hard, hurt, pain, sad, longing for Jim, celebrations, visitors, bedtime. Sometimes I only ate to keep medications down.

There were setbacks and setups. Faithful family and friends tried to brighten mundane days. Because I was unable to fully function independently, my parents welcomed me back to their home. I had missed our first Christmas together. I no longer shared our home with Jim. The beach honeymoon would never be. The game of dodge ball against life just became tougher and I didn't have my teammate anymore. I couldn't fathom what would come next. I had no idea I would be in their home, sharing this experience, for the next 3 months.

Heavenly Father,

We know there is an enemy prowling around, waiting to attack us. Please help us run to you and your Word as the greatest weapon against this enemy. Thank you for being a God of hope, love, healing, among many other things. Help us to trust your direction in our lives, and give us the strength to take the steps in your direction. Show us what to do, and count on us faithfully doing it.

In Jesus name I pray,

Amen

Chapter 3 Questions for Reflection:

1. What life-changing event meant to destroy you has God turned around for good? *(see Genesis 50:20)*

2. In times of struggle, what is your greatest weapon against the enemy?

3. Think of a time in your life dreams or plans didn't happen. How has God taken you in a different direction?

4. Read 2 Corinthians 4:4

Jim stole everyone's heart, including mine, as he cried when I walked down the aisle.

Just pronounced husband and wife!

My dad (Ken), mom (Kay), me, Jim, sister (Kasey), and brother-in-law (Troy)

Jim and I were so in love and ready to share our lives together! Here we are standing beside his precious 1989 Chevy Cameo. It was our wedding vehicle!

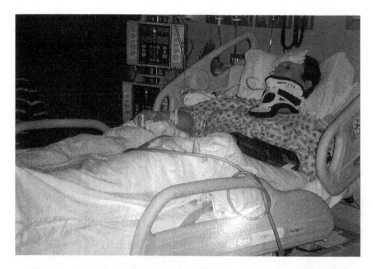

This picture was taken on December 19, 2011, the day after our accident. I had already had some surgeries, but still had a few more to go. I was in a medically-induced coma.

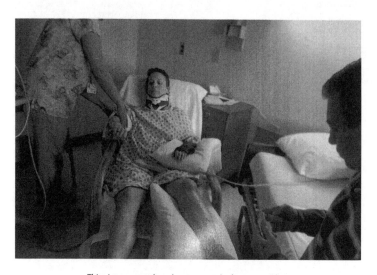

This picture was taken about one week after our accident.
Although not a pretty picture, it shows God's healing

CHAPTER FOUR

HOME

"Be grateful for the home you have,
knowing that at this moment,
all you have is all you need."
– Sarah Ban Breathnach

I was seeking some semblance of normalcy. Normalcy unattainable after spending the past 7 ½ weeks living somewhere other than my home; living a life that did not seem my own. I couldn't see it then, but living with my parents after Woodlawn supplied exactly what I needed. Modifications made to their home turned a two-story house into a ranch that met all my medical needs solely on the first floor. Once again, the Minerva community and others drew close to love one of their own. Family and friends all wanted to lend a hand in any way they could.

Wisely, doctors progressively lessened my medication intake throughout this time. Suffering withdrawal is not an enjoyable experience. There are many outlets for escaping grief in unhealthy ways, but thankfully, I could not participate. Because of physical limitations I was unable to stay busy to fill the missing void. I could feel myself trying to numb, but didn't have the stamina to battle numbness all day and night. My best attempt at escaping was telling myself, "If I don't grieve, it will seem like it didn't happen." But there were too many physical reminders, piled on top of missing Jim every minute. As much as I tried to metaphorically hide, my parents always found me.

I had multiple risk factors, and was diagnosed as experiencing PTSD. I had all the symptoms—flashbacks, nightmares, sleeplessness, guilt, dissociation, and memory gaps related to the accident. I was frustrated from all the battles, and grieving declared my defeat.

Some days offered more to celebrate than others. It wasn't normal to cheer because I dressed with little help, but become physically unraveled at not being able to put my contacts in my eyes. It wasn't normal for my parents to praise my independence when I hopped to the restroom on my own, but then have to cut up my food to eat. How do you help another adult shower with dignity? This is normal, even cute, when you are a toddler. Not so much as a prideful 32 year old. It felt severely out of sorts. We tried to navigate by creating systematic routines.

Mentally, we organized the day into manageable chunks. The morning chunk was for waking, breakfast, medications, and business. "Business" mostly meant dealing with medical bills, doctors, and lawyers. My mom, the ultimate caregiver, shone as hostess, secretary, nutritionist, chef, nurse, and business manager. Dad hurried home from school for the afternoon and evening chunks. In addition to checking in during lunch break, he helped us with the PM chunk that included therapy, shower, dinner, bedtime.

Through it all, we missed Jim. We all so sadly missed Jim. We discovered we could be okay together in this different storm. Just okay: nothing more, nothing less. Through the discomfort, sadness, awkwardness, and frustrations, we were making it—one day at a time.

We found reasons to smile and laugh. Imagine my dad popping wheelies in the snow with me in the wheelchair—our personal comedienne.

Suddenly, and for the first time since the accident, I had thoughts of someone outside of myself. My parents were caring for me so much, who was caring for them?

How was my family holding it together? What about my friends? What about Jim's family and friends? They lost someone, too! Their lives changed, too! The empathy that comes with realizing how loss impacts so many people can be overwhelming. But, recognizing how many others had same longing for Jim led to the first time I didn't feel alone. I clung to those willing to walk this path alongside me.

Physical and occupational therapy at Concorde Therapy Group in Alliance, Ohio became a new arena for me. Besides connecting to its abundance of great people, I felt beyond blessed physically to have advanced more than I thought I could, maybe even more than medically probable. The therapists never pitied me, they empathized. They got to know me quickly and learned how to challenge and support this part of the journey. I took my first steps in February 2012, regaining limited use of my left hand over 3 months later. We never looked back. Although things would be different, I could go as far as I was willing to work. Improving, although grueling and painful, was a contagious spark, and fed a competitive hunger I had cultivated in my years of sports, coaching, and personal growth. I felt challenged, driven. Therapy gave me a mission to be more than a sad story. My mentality shifted from "I can't do it" to "I want to do it." Through successes and support, I gained momentum.

May 2012 brought gigantic leaps and forward progress. I began driving again, albeit hesitantly. With some apprehension, I moved out of my parents' house and back into the apartment that Jim and I shared. I felt the world become accessible again, life returning to my fingertips, with worship and fellowship at Cornerstone Church, and enjoyable time with friends and family. I wasn't able to return to full duty at work just yet. So, cane in hand, I volunteered in my own classroom a few hours a week. My family urged me to enter Gentle Shepherd Counseling Center, in North Canton, Ohio. I humbly did so, and quickly realized the many benefits of a counseling relationship. I continue today. Progress, however painful, unfamiliar, discouraging, sad, unwanted, or slow is most appreciated when you've been held back.

August 1, 2012, nearly eight months after the accident, I was cleared to return to full duty school teaching. I worked so hard to get back to work. (Oh the irony.) I soon realized that though my job stayed the same, I had changed. Everything had changed. And life could never be the same.

My school district emails a newsletter for all employees each Friday called "The Weekly Guide." In November, 2012, near what would have been my first wedding anniversary, I wrote a feature that newsletter. Allow me to share a portion of that piece. "A friend at recently passed on the story of the palm tree and, in doing so, told me that I was like a palm tree! I had never heard this story before, so I dug a little deeper. As it turns out, a palm tree never breaks during high winds or storms. Rather it bends from side to side, and sometimes will bend so much that its leaves touch the ground. Additionally, the palm tree has its greatest growth spurt after facing the challenges and discomforts of the high winds and storms. But, when the weather is nice, the palm tree just lets its leaves blow and does nothing. The tree does not grow when it's comfortable and unchallenged.

My personal storm blew in last December 18th. I quickly learned that this bending process is not fun, without challenge, or discomfort. I am thankful for God, family and friends that have stood in this storm with me so far. I have many thankful, blessed stories I would love to share given the time, but one recently came to life. I needed to have an uncomfortable, tough conversation with the teaching team I work with every day. As I gathered all my strength and controlled gut-wrenching tears, I opened up about my storm. I told them that physically healing and emotionally grieving has been extremely rough, but these two months back at work seemed harder than anything I had ever experienced working before. I asked them for their help, grace, prayers and understanding through this time. I received nothing but sup-

port and love. I am so thankful for them. Whatever your storm may be right now, I tell you with a heavy heart that is still bending, when the storm clears, you will be all the better for it."

Heavenly Father,

Thank you for creating us like the palm tree. Thank you for your presence in our lives and the many provisions you give us. Thank you for placing the right people in our lives when we needed them most. We know this world is not our forever home, but may our lives and love for others continuously glorify you.

In Jesus name I pray,

Amen

Chapter 4 Questions for Reflection:

1. What is one circumstance that has given you a new mission for your life?

2. Think about the story of the palm tree. Identify a season that almost broke you, but instead you have grown. *(see Romans 5:3-5)*

3. Read Psalm 107

CHAPTER FIVE

MOVING FORWARD

"In struggle and chaos, the next step is still our
choice. For that, let us be grateful and bold."
– Brendon Burchard

Sitting on the patio of our condo overlooking the ocean, I am awestruck at its beauty. It's such an intense love, what the ocean and I share. If you can silence the surrounding sounds, focus away from distractions, it can be the greatest of all teachers. As they move forward, the waves never know what they will meet when they reach the shore; yet they diligently return every time. Realistically, I am aware that everyone does not grieve, hurt, heal, or move forward similarly, but I want to be like a wave diligently pressing into the unknown every day. It requires conscious choices, strength, and perseverance.

As a young widow, pressing into the unknown began immediately, with no other option. I felt I had lost everything. I looked for one reason--one small reason--to get up in the morning. Though challenging to find on many days, once discovered that one small reason had the strength of an elephant as it carried me forward the entire day. I took small steps, one day at a time, amid the paradox of life seemingly ending, stopping—but, then, despite it all, the sun rises, giving light to a new day. Reasons just to get up began to morph into choices to consciously move forward. In *Every Day Deserves a Chance*, author Max Lucado writes, "Days are the bite-sized portions of life, the God-designed segments of life-management. God meets daily needs daily and miraculously." Some days, I found myself sure-footed along the weary path of moving forward, making positive choices-turned-actions along the way. On the other days, I did not feel so sure-footed, and leaned heavily on my crutches. My experience has taught that crutches can either be God-centered, or centered in an underlying tone of defeat and complacency. More later about the God-centered crutches, but I'm convinced that going through life disconnected from God is like going through the grocery store without a list—and hungry! Flashy temptations catch our eye and cause us to lose focus. We rely on ourselves, spend more than we should, and we settle. Stick with God, and stick to your grocery list.

Moving forward warrants our best effort. As the great distance track runner, Steve Prefontaine, said, "To give anything less than your best is to sacrifice the gift!" It's a step towards health to move forward. Mentally and emotionally it's healthier to talk about things, seek help, be authentic, work through, and these all lead to moving forward. We will be tempted to numb, fill, be busy, be fake, isolate—these temptations lead to being stuck and even more miserable. The devil has his way with stuck people. He finds great pleasure attacking me in the early morning, when he assumes I am groggy, defenseless, fearing the day ahead. But God subtly declares victory by the rise of the sun and the breath in our lungs.

Each morning I make a series of declarations for the day. I can't take credit for this idea, but it has been so helpful to me that I must pass it on. A few of the declarations are: Jesus is first, I am His daughter, I am empowered and equipped, I will love people, I will not compare myself to others, I will give myself grace, I will never give up. I've found that when I miss making these declarations, my "one plate" of burden and responsibility feels more like a "buffet." Insecurity creeps in, I miss joyful moments, I lose focus and perspective, people are too much to handle.

Physically our bodies are designed to move forward. For months I only used the right side of my body—oh the pain, challenges, humility of that time: hopping on one leg to slowly get around, depending on one arm and hand to do what two had normally done every day. But still I pushed on. Our bodies are wonderful machines of adapting, overcoming, compensating. Playing through pain is not for the faint of heart, but it's necessary and rewarding.

God does not call us victims—or even survivors; rather He calls us victorious and wants us to thrive. 1 Peter 5:10 says, "In His kindness God called you to share in His eternal glory by means of Christ Jesus. So after you have suffered a little while, He will restore, support, and strengthen you, and He will place you on a firm foundation." I used to feel that victory meant winning something, feeling a sense of accomplishment, or standing on a podium with a medal around my neck. It was a finish line, something to strive for. That's the coach in me, the competitor in me, even the immaturity in me talking. I now know that victory is perseverance in the face of a worldly beat-down, gaining something valuable to Christ, learning something that grows me closer to Him in this season—and carries me through the next. Victory is steadfastly looking squarely at the enemy's devices—fear, bitterness, insecurity, obstacles--and telling Satan every minute that he will not defeat anyone who has claimed victory in Christ. Proverbs 21:31 declares, "The horse is made ready for the day of the battle, but victory rests with the Lord." I'm not attempting to downplay the challenges, but instead inspire you to fight the temptation to go into survival mode, to hang your head in the gloom of a muddy season and just get by. In *It's Your Time*, Joel Osteen writes "We're supposed to break through to a new level, to more of God's favor, to increase, to promotion."

Please remember that you are not moving forward in effort to leave things behind or pretend to be better than someone else. You are moving forward to honor your past, to grow through and grow ahead.

For me, moving out of the apartment Jim and I shared was a big step in growing through. The associations with that apartment had a great hold on me—trying their best to keep me stuck. Obligation, discouragement, and loneliness had run their course, but there was so much fear in moving forward to a new place without Jim. Isn't it funny that sometimes staying unpacked where you are is so much easier, comfortable, and less fearful than packing up and moving forward to the new, healthier, and different? Why do we sometimes choose to be comfortably miserable rather than uncomfortably joyful? When I made the choice to move, things fell into place quickly. God had his hands in preparing the right time, right place, right people, and putting in the right offer. I had wonderful help, and got quickly settled. I have comfortably lived in my new home over four years now. Feelings of safety and new memories fill its walls. Ironically, it's a home I love, but Jim would not have loved it. That fact actually makes me smile as I write it. Moving helped me turn to the next page in my story.

Two years after the accident, I arrived at the point where I was satisfied doing life on my own. Yet shortly thereafter God placed the desire for marriage and family on my heart again. We all have hopes and desires. Often they aren't fulfilled in the status quo. As people, we want better. To BE better. But this does not mean we aren't content.

One evening during a treadmill workout, I thought deeply about contentment. Contentment is a choice, one that has to be chosen daily. Contentment means discerning between wants and needs, authentic and superficial, security in Christ (and insecurity in anything else), trust and control. It's the balance between honoring your past, working hard for your future, while being totally present in the moment. We are not limited by what others have, like, think, or do successfully. There's room enough for us all. That's not boastful or prideful. Jesus loves us unconditionally—died for us—has more than enough grace and forgiveness for all our shortcomings—has a purposeful plan designed for us—has the best timing for us—equips and empowers us—type of way.

However, when you go through something so traumatically life-changing, the world really starts to look like an ugly reflection in the mirror. Honestly, it took me some time to truly be content in my present. I can speak to the battle for contentment in real time because I am still fighting it.

Philippians 4:12-13 speaks about contentment in this way, "I know what it is to be in need, and I know what it is to have plenty. I have learned the secret of being content in any and every situation, whether well fed or hungry, whether living in plenty or in want. I can do all this through Him who gives me strength."

I'd had my forever man, but tragically, our forever was cut short. I have made the choice in my singleness to prepare to be the best wife and mother possible. I want a new relationship, a new friendship, a teammate, and I desire to be those to someone else as well. I haven't forgotten all the beauty love brings. I pray every day, thanking God for the husband and family he is preparing for me, that he continues to prepare me to be the best wife and mother I can be. I am dating now because I am ready, not just because I desire to.

I now feel adept in moving forward. I know it's not an identical journey for everyone. I know all too well that it is not easy, quick, or pretty. On what was the five year anniversary of the accident, I woke up greeted by the devil. My body ached and I was crying before I'd even opened my eyes. Mustering up all I had, I prayed and invited God into the day. I did this because I desired a change, I desired to be better. Some people don't desire to be better at all. Some people think that appearing better is actually becoming better. But for me, desiring to be truly better was a nonnegotiable after the accident. I reflected on how through the accident I really began to respect growth and the process of moving forward. That's when I learned that trying to make myself superficially look better would never be fulfilling or enough. I will stumble. I may go slowly at times, but I will never give up my pursuit of authentic health and progress.

You may find, on your own road to true health and well-being, a path littered with difficulty, opposition, and doubt. Carry on anyway. People may not always support or agree with the better, different you. Love them anyway. Cling to the good and the real in people. One of the toughest parts of loss is how to embrace the different in your life when the rest of the world stays the same. Sometimes, even still, I weep, desperately longing for the life I might have had, the life I hoped for. But I don't stay there. I choose to EMBRACE THE DIFFERENT.

The honest truth is, life goes on regardless. A blessed life does not always mean an easy one. This life will be hard for many reasons. Sometimes we are the cause, sometimes others hold that distinction. But, if we are Christ-followers, we can look back at hard times in our lives we thought we wouldn't survive, and be able to trace God's faithfulness. We can use His past provisions to lift us through our current challenging times. 1 Thessalonians 5:16-18 says, "Always be joyful. Never stop praying. Be thankful in all circumstances, for this is God's will for you who belong to Christ Jesus." God loves you and created you for a purpose. You are strong, like a palm tree, growing in adversity. Be that palm tree—you are worth it.

As this chapter closes, one final thought: Recently, I transferred the diamond from my original engagement ring into a new setting. As I enjoy its beauty, the ring now symbolizes more beyond the love Jim and I shared; the love I still have for him. It symbolizes that change can be a beautiful thing. The diamond that survived the accident, in which almost everything else was broken or destroyed, is firmly embracing the different setting it has been given; yet it shines still—strong and confident, forever and always the precious gem it was created to be.

Heavenly Father,

If we had to rely on our own strength to move forward, we would tire and fail. We are so thankful that you never grow weary of doing good in our lives. You continue to bless us, undeservedly. May we always remember that you are our firm foundation and to rest securely in that truth. In you, nothing is wasted and we have purpose.

In Jesus name I pray,

Amen

Chapter 5 Questions for Reflection:

1. What crutches do you lean on when you lose your footing in life?
   (see Proverbs 3:5-6)

2. What is one area of your life that has you in its grip and keeps you from moving forward?

3. Read Job 17:9

4. Do you have a version of morning declarations? If so, what are they?

CHAPTER SIX

TRUE TRANSFORMATION

*"There's no life so shattered that it
cannot be restored."*
– Dieter F. Uchtdorf

Healing has been my part-time job over the last few years. God has turned this struggle into a gift. Although this story has not followed my script, my Redeemer has been right beside me restoring and re-building me. I earnestly tell you, when your desire to mend outweighs your desire to end, that is when true growth and transformation begins.

I need to start by explaining some of the ugliness in my desire to end following the accident.

My counselor at Gentle Shepherd lovingly offered words of comfort during one of our first sessions together, saying that I should picture a huge painting, and at that point I could only see what was pressed against my nose. Bitterly I replied that I didn't like art.

People observed I was "different." To me, that meant that I had failed, lost, was pitied, wasn't good enough to be labeled normal. My pendulum of self-reliance had swung from being Miss Independent to Mrs. Dependent. I was so insecure, and even angrier because of that insecurity. The past was too painful, the present was unbearable, the future seemed unattainable. Battles between self-pity and self-entitlement were fought on a daily basis. Looking back, the gloves were always on. Every day was battle-filled. Unable to see any perspective other than my own, I became self-centered and small. I played the victim, seeking answers to why this happened to me and where was God? I tried to control and hold on to some things so tight, determined to never lose anything again. Life was hard, but teaching seemed easy, so I compartmentalized life. I was a great actor. I was one person in one place, and another person in another place. Not fitting in, no boundaries, not knowing who I really was made me look in the mirror at an unfamiliar face. Hiding within myself -- isolated, lonely, different.

Can you believe that I was actually glad I was so physically hurt? Jim lost his life. If I wasn't going to die, the least I could do was physically suffer in mine. I believed I was a burden to my parents, the rest of my family, my friends –everything and everyone. I began having nightmares about the accident. Many nights I lie in bed shivering, sweat-soaked, and defeated. My weak prayers were simply telling God that I couldn't do this, didn't want to do this, and He should make this end. I didn't want to wake up!

Clearly, I've awakened every morning since then. Triumphantly now! As I have gone through trauma therapy and counseling, I haven't had a single nightmare in over three years! Most importantly, working through it all enticed my desire to mend. My tried and true recipe for mending requires three ingredients: going into a deeper relationship with Christ, allowing God to work in me— and participating, and being grateful for the gifts.

Talking to God and spending time in His word helped me distinguish between His voice and the voice of the enemy talking. I cancelled out the voice of the enemy. I found such contentment in Jesus and living each day knowing that tomorrow is not promised. I already talked to myself quite a bit; now I find it necessary to talk to God more. I am at a place in my healing and growth where I am more openly honest about myself than ever before.

Being stripped down to nothing but your bare bones is similar to a tornado coming and ravaging a house down to the foundation. There is much rebuilding ahead, but the foundation stands firm. God has faithfully rebuilt my security in Him. Amazingly, God can transform an angry, bitter heart into a heart that has passion for Him and His priorities. Max Lucado, in *It's Not About Me,* writes, "Your pain has a purpose. Your problems, struggles, heartaches, and hassles cooperate toward one end--the glory of God."

I have several tattoos. I know how to conceal them when it seems appropriate or necessary. I see being angry, insecure, bitter, petty, miserable like having a tattoo. You can cover those emotions up when it seems appropriate, but they will still be there. Allowing God to work in you, identifying the thoughts, feelings, and triggers can help develop healthier actions and choices. My bitterness has been turned into relationship. Anger has turned into compassion. Self-pity into empathy. I am more God-centered, less self-centered. He is turning a hard heart that thought love was lost forever into an open heart that will love forever. Brokenness and weakness can be turned into strength. You can only know healing after you first experience pain. Struggle gains wisdom. There is courage in being uncomfortable.

The gloves that I'd worn for so long slowly came off. In Jesus, I found it vital to let go of some old things to make room for the new. I am learning to pick my battles wisely, pray for discernment, and realize not everything needs my hands in it, my ears listening to it, my words said about it, or my emotional reaction to it. I trust God more, and get out of the way to let God do what needs to be done. Pastor John Piper says, "When everything in life is stripped away except God, and we trust Him more because of it, this is gain, and He is glorified!" Remember the painting I was directed to imagine? God sees the whole work of art—and he's a great artist. God will do what I can't, in His time. I want to be obedient, and do what I should.

The lenses through which I see the world have drastically changed, as has my perspective--deeper, intentional, stronger, bigger. The greatest of all views came when I clearly saw that knowing God is so much better than knowing answers. I can look back and see that God has loved, healed, comforted, and blessed me, and he continues to still do so. With God, we know we are loved and beautiful, so there is no room to hoard and hide our ugly. We can love ourselves because we love the one who loves us so much. That is one of the most amazing realizations I've come to experience. It overwhelms me.

I was swimming with one of my best friends, Linnea, and her children. Her oldest, Caleb, an intelligent, kindhearted, adventurous boy was tempted to make a poor behavior choice with some other children. Looking at the other children, then back at his mother, he walked away, making a good choice, then joyfully returned to play in the pool. Like Caleb, I've often been tempted to make a bad choice--and many times have succumbed—but by looking to Jesus Christ and His forgiveness, I've joyfully returned to the pool of life. Such freedom and joy comes from being obedient.

People calling me "different" now is a compliment of growth. When I'm not honest about my grief, it makes a liar out of me. I can't be the same now as I was before, because everything that is not mending is essentially ending. Been there, done that. In *Get Out of that Pit,* Beth Moore writes that "You are a much neater person healed than you would have been well--wealth of experience makes you rich." The past becomes less painful. It feels good to remember and share memories with people. As I become whole, see the connections, and transform from the inside out, it is possible to honor what I've lost and what I have now. There is nothing worth going backwards.

I don't know the certainty of the future, but I'm moving forward anyway. I know I need to continue growing and developing. I know I am loved greatly by my family and friends. I know in all things that God works for the good of those that love and follow Him. Over the last five years, I have grown wiser, stronger, more vulnerable, and authentic. I am more obedient in my daily walk with Jesus. I love more deeply and wholeheartedly. I am more compassionate and present. God is faithful.

I'm often told people don't know how I've come this far, how I've been able to continue. People frequently say they couldn't do it. Trust me, I did not choose this path. I've done more rebuilding, experiencing, working, changing, and growing than I ever thought was needed in my life. God's favor has brought me through. There is no quitting now. I've come too far. Humanly, I am still struggling against my old self. I experience hard work, mistakes, tough days, and pain. Paul spoke to the Philippians about joy and pressing on in Philippians 3:12-16, "I don't mean to say that I have already achieved these things or that I have already reached perfection. But I press on to possess that perfection for which Christ Jesus first possessed me. No, dear brothers and sisters, I have not achieved it, but I focus on this one thing: Forgetting the past and looking forward to what lies ahead, I press on to reach the end of the race and receive the heavenly prize for which God, through Christ Jesus, is calling us. Let all who are spiritually mature agree on these things. If you disagree on some point, I believe God will make it plain to you. But we must hold on to the progress we have already made!"

I would never want anyone else to go through what I've experienced, but my faith, strength, perspective, wisdom--people *would* benefit from that. I am so grateful to my God who calls me loved, favored, accepted, forgiven. He is ever present, ever hopeful. I am thankful for Him who never grows weary, because I sure do. Walking with Jesus is like most things in life -- if you are hungry enough for it, you will eat as much of it as you can. Jeff Hanna, a friend and pastor, has allowed me to use his words as my life motto, "God will not fail, I will not quit." Believe God will not fail you either, then never quit!

Heavenly Father,

Open our hearts and minds to be transformed by you. We faithfully trust that you will not fail us, and we know that we need to keep persevering through the race. May we continue to live in the Holy Spirit. Thank you for meeting us where we are and growing us in you.

In Jesus name I pray,

Amen

Chapter 6 Questions for Reflection:

1. How have you been transformed by the Holy Spirit? *(see Colossians 3:1-12)*

2. Write your life motto.

3. Read Titus 3:4-5

CHAPTER SEVEN

FORGIVENESS

"Forgiveness isn't approving what happened.
It's choosing to rise above it."
– Robin Sharma

Driving to the Stark County Court of Common Pleas with my parents felt like it took days, though it really only took thirty minutes. Special parking, people eyes following me, moving unsteadily using a walker, wearing "dress clothes" compared to the lounge wear I'd worn for the past few months. Instead of celebrating my birthday in March of 2012, I was facing the man who killed my husband and caused my current condition. It was such an awkward day! I hoped that I would finally be able to forgive him and move on.

I remember sitting down, and listening to the driver who hit us. As he read his statement, seemingly genuine, sincere, remorseful, I was barely able to hear him. He had limped in with a broken ankle. A broken ankle? That's all that happened to him---he broke an ankle! I was still unable to use my left hand or arm. I walked only with assistance. I was unable to get my wedding rings to even fit my hand. My husband was dead. I had been through months of pain and therapy, longing desperately for my husband. My life was ruined, and he broke his ankle! Not fair! I was at some point beyond anger, and numb. No forgiveness was given that day.

Not forgiving him seemed to honor the fact that I hated the accident and disapproved of the driver—a validation of sorts. I wanted a quick fix for the hurt, and felt that if I forgave him, I could avoid pain. He did receive thirteen years in prison by taking a plea deal. However, I knew there was no winner. Everyone had already lost something big.

The online resource, Wikipedia, defines forgiveness as "the intentional process by which a victim undergoes a change in feelings and attitude regarding an offense, let's go of negative emotions such as vengefulness, with an increased ability to wish the offender well." I have spoken to people who have lost someone. They have either blamed God or didn't know who to blame. My knowing who to blame only gave me someone to focus on. There are three parts to that definition and it took me a really long time to fully forgive the driver who hit us.

My feelings and attitudes about the accident began to change as I continued my counseling, received the correct medication for PTSD, and invited God in to transform me. It was uncomfortable, but refreshing, to view the driver in a new way. He was a 23-year-old who made a horrible choice to drive drunk. His decision led to a devastating, life-changing event. There is no amount of harm I could cause him that would bring Jim back. I couldn't make a different choice for him; I could, however, make a different choice for me.

But to wish him well? That, my friends, took some time. But I am grateful that I can finally, honestly say that I now have forgiven him. I genuinely hope he is doing the work to change his life, and learning from a very hard experience. We all have only one life and it should not be wasted.

I am often asked how I could forgive him. Forgiving him has given me a peace and freedom because I don't have to play the victim anymore. He does not have that power over me. I can now be victorious. Pastor Brenda Young writes, "You can hold on to blame, or you can have peace. You can't have both." Forgiveness really had more to do with me than with him. I am a grudge-holder. I could blame this characteristic on everything other than what it really is. I could blame genetics, my gender, age— anything really. But I've learned that just as I allowed God to work in me for forgiveness of the driver, I also needed to allow God to work in me, to remove my grudge-holding tendencies so I could forgive myself and others.

I know that we have an important part to play in God's plan. But I sometimes want God to play the part I have directed for Him. I often ask forgiveness for getting that backwards. I ask His forgiveness for my excuse of busyness, my know-it-all attitude, less-than-loving thoughts of others, my stubbornness, my people pleasing, my anger, and my impatience for prayers being answered in my time.

Forgiveness holds the freedom to pick up what God has for us now that our hands are free from the bitterness we were holding onto. I've discovered that the things that have held me down the longest are mostly the things that I've been unwilling to release. I've also found that I can't fully embrace and enjoy the freedoms of Christ when I am making myself a slave. We try to walk so many fine lines between loyalty or obligation, compassion or controlling, being driven by God or doing the driving myself, yes or no.

The Bible records Jesus' Parable of the Unforgiving Debtor in Matthew 18:21-35. A king forgave a servants' debt only to have that servant turn around and be un-forgiving to his fellow servant who owed him. The king, unable to comprehend that the servant just forgiven of his debt could not forgive another man's debt, then had the servant put in prison and tortured until he paid his entire debt. Intrinsically we are tortured when we don't forgive others. Do not confuse whom you punish when you choose to not forgive. As much as we may want the wrongdoer to suffer, we are the ones that become bitter, miserable, and unloving. We are unconditionally loved and forgiven by our Father God for all the sin that we do. Jesus said in Luke 7:47, "I tell you, her sins—and they are many—have been forgiven, so she has shown me much love. But a person who is forgiven little shows only little love." Shouldn't I then extend forgiveness to others? I can still disapprove of the accident, be authentic about that, be sad that it happened, but I can't hold onto the blame and bitterness. This is a lesson I continue to learn and live.

Recently, I was eating with a few friends at a restau-rant and was talking about how I'd lost fifty pounds over the last year. Completely vulnerable and honest, I spoke about the transformation of being unhealthy, finding comfort from food, and filling my head with lies about all the things I couldn't do. I used to feel so incapable, stag-nant, and stuck. I told them that my body used to physi-cally ache more than it does now. I was praising how big our God is. I told them that exercising has provided refuge to unwind from the school day, let any other stressors off the hook, talk to God in prayer, and competitively challenge myself in many different ways. Having a multitasking mind that's always thinking, dreaming, problem-solving, and reflecting, exercise has given me enough focus to rest. It's been very hard, I have worked so hard at it and I feel so much better for it. As I was finishing with tear-filled eyes, one of my friends said, "If you had a life with a husband and kids then you wouldn't be losing weight and exercising."

Frankly, there are far worse things to say to me—that I would much rather hear. I immediately wanted to rant back in anger. I could feel my face get hot. I wanted to say, "I want marriage and family again. I had a marriage once, but I didn't cause the accident, want the accident, and don't like the accident. I'm trying my best where I am. I don't have this all figured out. And…you're just mean and jealous." Instead of telling her all that, I cried uncontrollably and left the restaurant without even paying for the food I didn't get to eat. I'm an introvert and we are prone to withdraw and grow cold when we get hurt. I can surely hold a grudge. I don't claim to be confrontational, I'm secretly hopeful that most disagreements can be solved by prayer, bubble baths, and big hugs. But sometimes confrontation it is necessary. My friend and I have since talked, reconciled the real issue, and reconnected. It is possible to still hold others accountable for their actions while forgiving them. Sometimes I struggle with forgiveness, as my pride or hurt gets in the way. I pray often that I am able to have the state of mind to forgive others. Trusting God, I pray to give Him the right to take care of justice.

It boils down to perspective. Even with the best intentions, I am still often in need of forgiveness, both knowingly and unknowingly, by others. This perspective always gets me back on track. I must forgive as I am forgiven. Not forgiving chains us to the past and destroys us from the inside-out; but forgiveness frees us in the present, heals, grows us, allows us to move forward to the future. You have to acknowledge, face directly, what you are really holding onto, in order to truly let it go. It's ugly. It's hard. It's not a one-time deal. It's not a quick fix. Remember: the servant that is forgiven much, forgives much.

Heavenly Father,

May we glorify you by forgiving others as you have forgiven us. You are the justice-giver and the final authority. In you, we are set free to pick up all you have in store for us with two open, willing hands.

In Jesus name I pray,

Amen

Chapter 7 Questions for reflection:

1. Are you a grudge-holder?

2. Who/what do you need to forgive in order to be free and at peace?

3. Read Luke 15:11-32

4. Read Colossians 3:13-15

CHAPTER EIGHT

PURPOSEFUL PEOPLE

"A friend is one that knows you
as you are, understands where you have
been, accepts what you have become,
and still, gently allows you to grow."
– William Shakespeare

Being hurt by people is like rising gasoline pric-es—we complain about it, but it is a reality we will live with no matter the cost. I've been on the receiving end of people's intimidation, feelings of infuriation, insecurities, inaccurate assumptions, indecent treatment. People have called me names, critiqued my life choices, given advice they themselves do not follow. I have been talked at and talked about. I've listened as others cut down my situation only to make theirs stand a little taller.

There was a period after the accident where some of my relationships became one- sided, unhealthy, and needed some repair. Sadly, I discovered that not all people really wanted me to get better. Some friends did not like the changed me. A changing, different me was too much for them. For some, subtly, the pity they once felt for me had now turned to envy for progress made. I found this period very difficult as I was used to having a big, diverse group of valued friends in my life, and people leaving that group brought back a familiar fear of loss.

While continuing to grow, heal, and be transformed during these periods, I learned that one-sided relationships, no matter how much effort you put in, start and end the same way—one-sided. Sometimes people not liking you has very little to do with you at all. There is something going on with them. Satan can use people to hurt you, but that doesn't make them bad people. It's so crucial to pray for them, and to pray protection over your own heart. It must be guarded. Push a loyal person far enough, and the time will come to set up healthy boundaries for unhealthy people: Emotional, mental, and physical boundaries. I've learned that when you try to establish boundaries with people when you are angry, then it becomes more of a great wall separating you from everyone. That's unhealthy. I've done it. Boundaries must allow you to love someone while allowing you to also love yourself. Give yourself permission to not be around negative people. Gaining new relationships can be absolutely appealing because the new friend naturally loves you where you are and supports your growth. Wes Angelozzi says, "Go and love someone exactly as they are. And then watch how quickly they transform into the greatest, truest version of themselves. When one feels seen and appreciated in their own essence, one is instantly empowered."

We live in such a competitive, comparing society. We can be attention seekers, only listening to someone to be heard ourselves. We are easily distracted, and equate being busy with being purposeful and important. Social media can only feed those beasts if we let it. It's easy to get caught in the trap of seeing someone else's highlight film while sitting in what we wish were our deleted scenes. It's an online battle against pity, entitlement, popularity, competition. It's a place that makes an art of inflating mole hills into mountains. There's no accountability. We miscommunicate through posts and pictures and passive-aggressive commentary. We are sometimes seemingly closer with friends that are states away than we are with friends that are streets away. Get out of the trap. Monitor your media, enjoy social media for what it is, but spend your time on real life relationships with real life people.

I'm regularly annoyed at how easy it is to take other people's opinions of me as fact. There are times when I struggle to drown out that loud voice telling me I am what my insecurities say I am. People are going to say and think what they want. When you can, arm them with the truth. Then the worst thing they can say is that they don't like you. Love them anyway. A friend once told me that when you know where your friends are in your life, you can't expect them to be anywhere else. Truly, no two people are running the same race anyway. If God has a specific, purposeful plan for our lives, then why would we need to spend it comparing and competing with others? We can either help each other or hurt each other on our races. Galatians 5:26 says, "Let us not become conceited, or provoke one another, or be jealous of one another."

It's so healthy to remember that everything in life is connected. God's calling for us lies in the interdependence of our lives. As I said, I'm an introvert, this makes me socially awkward at times, but that does not give me permission to be an isolated hermit. Whether or not we like our past, it connects to our present. Whether or not we like the things that have happened to us, those things connect to who we are and who we will become. Whether or not some people are hard to get along with, or even attack us, we are still connected to each other.

The people that challenge me to be my best, the people that unknowingly get me back on the path when I wander off, all have a few things in common. Not acting any better or worse than anyone they interact with, they treat everyone with respect. By realizing that people are not all the same, they treat others the way the *others* want to be treated. They are diverse and different than me. They give without expectation of return. Investors, they connect and focus on people. They overcome, yet ask for help. Good communicators, they are authentic, secure, and comfortable with themselves. Honorable and passionate, they walk their talk even when no one is watching. On this journey, it's been pointed out multiple times, "You just don't know what you don't know." Only when you know better can you be better. That's why it's so important to closely evaluate the circle of people you are spending a lot of time around. Proverbs 27:9 says, "The heartfelt counsel of a friend is as sweet as perfume and incense."

I am praying for my teachable heart. I am a student of life—everyone in my life is a teacher of something. There are different types of friendship, and sometimes friendships change. We could all sometimes kindly ask for a redo of a comment made, a moment done, an action committed. On rough days, people make mistakes, but most do try. With expectation comes disappointment.

When I get caught up in disappointment with people, it is a good time to look for the good in them or check my own heart.

An accountability question I often ask myself is "What am I teaching others?" I want to be held accountable, but give myself grace. Reading the previous sentence again, it seems that one I hold on to so tightly while the other slips right through. It's so hard to let myself off the hook sometimes. It's so hard for me to show myself kindness, grace, and forgiveness. I'm thinking if I have these struggles within myself, that's probably the reason I struggle giving it to others at times. I pray often for God's guidance, strength, and wisdom to change where it is needed. This takes time, sometimes a break from the friendship, some time alone to reflect, refresh. Trust me, over the past few years there have been many things that I've needed to change. I am certain there will be more in the future, too!

I'm a closet people-pleaser. My bark is way worse than my bite. It disgusts me, but I feel empowered by acknowledging it. I don't think people-pleasing is always evil, but the problem is in the fact that we can't focus on pleasing both people and God at the same time. It has taken me some growth to truly realize that if we only follow the people that follow Christ, it will always be flawed because people are flawed. All of us. But if we follow Christ, He is and always will be perfect. I choose the one that is perfect. He is slowly delivering me from deep care regarding what other people think of me.

Did you know there's now a "smart" toothbrush that can tell us when to brush the other side of our mouth? Amusing, but true. Wouldn't it be nice if there was some type of daily device that told us how to run our relationships? I would benefit, rather than be left to my own doing.

Remember the rising gasoline prices metaphor? The cost of being hurt by people is that we are also on the receiving God's unconditional love, support, encouragement, teachings, grace. Not to mentioned a few treasured friends'. I am my best around people that genuinely care, cover me with love and support; those who know and accept me with all my flaws, and know I'm enough even when I come up short. We dream and we do. They hold me accountable. They are loving, honest, intelligent, hard-working, and want to be their best. We make time for each other in all of our busyness. We live life, we laugh, and we seek a daily relationship with Christ. We don't drain the life out of each other. We don't quit. They can forgive mistakes and move on. They are already a few steps ahead of me doing the things well that I seek to do well, such as godly marriages, child-rearing, and daily living. Mutually, we make each other better, by sharing life together. We continue to learn, to grow, and to be joyful. I am loved, appreciated, respected by the best people on earth. It is an honor to love them. God's ears often hear my praises thanking Him for the family and friends in my life. Relationships are so important. We all want to feel like we are serve a purpose in the life of someone else. It takes an interdependent village -- we are not meant to do this life alone.

Heavenly Father,

Please help us to be life-givers, hope-dealers, and purposeful people to others for you. May our relationships please you and always grow towards you. It is so important to realize that we are not meant to do this life alone. May we praise you for the purposeful people in our lives.

In Jesus name I pray,

Amen

Chapter 8 Questions for reflection:

1. How does Matthew 28:19 relate to purposeful people and relationships?

2. Read John 17:22-26

3. Who draws the best out of you? What qualities do they all have in common?

4. What are you teaching others?

CHAPTER NINE

TRUTH to the MYTHS

*"There is a thing many people
outside your grief cannot understand:
that you have not simply lost one person, at
one point in time. You have lost their presence
in every aspect of your life. Your future has
changed as well as your now."*
– Megan Devine

There is no universal way to grieve, nor should there exist a universal expectation or obligation to grief. Grief does not fit into neat categories, stages, or order. It's chaotic, horrible, uniquely ours. When people tried to put my grieving process into a box, it only made

me feel hurried, out of sorts, and shamed for not con-
forming. There is such beauty, power, and compassion in
realizing that people grieve differently. I couldn't please
anyone, most certainly not myself. I have spent so much
time worrying about where I fit in life, then trying to do
the things to help me fit in. The truth is that God repeatedly tells us that we belong, that we are His. That, my
friends, is where we fit. But along this journey these are a
few of the grief "boxes" that I did not fit into. (*Note: There
are healthier ways to grieve than others, so please seek
professionals for guidance.)

My grief came in waves. In the beginning, those
waves held me under, which led to feelings of deep guilt,
despair, loneliness, loss, anger, insecurity. It was too much
to bear. Most days, I couldn't come up for air.

As I grew healthier in my grieving, I learned to tread
water. Counseling was a time of transition to invite God
in, to talk and to listen to Him more. I saw God work in me
and transform me. There was beauty as I began to better
choose my battles, and learned to let go of things that
were really holding me back. Guilt started to diminish,
and I was becoming present in the day. I found myself
laughing, and finding joyful moments in the day. I was
able to see the security in Jesus, and I wanted to live life. If
life is a battle of moments, it's necessary to win one battle
to get to the next.

I began a new hobby, surfing, and I started to apply some of the principles I was learning there to my day-to-day living. Good moments became good days. That does not mean I didn't fall or struggle, but I got back on the board to try again and move forward. Neither a novice, nor a pro, currently I am still surfing. I would much rather *grow* through struggles than just *go* through them. One is easier, but the other is life transforming. I continue to learn that "growing through" takes a heart continuously seeking Jesus, an abundance of grace, genuine gratitude, perseverance, a willing spirit for change and vulnerability, and an open mind. Sometimes I feel so strongly in my heart that things get a bit confusing and I get frustrated. But I must remember that God gave us a mind to balance out our heart. I must trust that and pray often for discernment.

Our world praises repression and calls it strength. I've been told multiple times "you are so strong" because people see me pulled together. They don't see me unraveled, crying on the floor, vulnerable, praying for God to help me through the next minute on this earth. When did ignoring grief become more beautiful, strong, or healthy than actually going through it? Many people go through grief alone, in silence, because others are so uncomfortable with it. Sometimes people only see the side of you they want to see. I've slowly realized that some people won't allow me to be broken or emotional around them. But it's not about asking permission to be yourself. It's about giving yourself permission to do so. Honestly, I am a strong person because I've had to be. I know where my strength comes from, and I'm stronger now because I've looked grief in the face and grown through it. The person I was six years ago could not handle the things that I have handled in the present. This is due to growth and strength through struggle. This process has connected me to the very sensitive, vulnerable, deeply emotional side of my life. It smoothes my rough edges, nudges me to love more completely, empathetically, authentically, transparently. I love that side of me. I know my emotions, know my crazy, and know my weaknesses. Windgate Lane says, "Grief is a nasty game of feeling the weakest you have ever felt and morphing it into the strongest person you will have to become." I'm ever thankful for the people in my life who were willing to be uncomfortable with me and love all sides of me so I could heal. I'm grateful for the people who stayed even though they could have left. Tears are not weakness, callousness is not strength. Take the time to experience grief, to grow through and grow forward.

Through and forward does not equal FORGET. As a matter of fact, I believe moving forward is the only way of truly remembering. Jim is one of my favorite people to both talk about and hear about. Recently on his birthday, I found my mind wandering to all the ways we would be celebrating his birthday together. Wandering aimlessly made me both angry and joyful in the same minute. I don't just miss Jim. I miss the way I felt with Jim, the way I was treated by him, the way I treated him. I miss our future together. I miss the way Jim's family felt with him as a son, brother, uncle, and friend. I miss the way my family felt with Jim and how they loved him and he loved them. I wept many times that day and missed Jim greatly. Truthfully, no cake perfectly baked and decorated, no expensive gift intentionally bought, not even my love wholeheartedly given is any competition for what heaven is offering him. Having those wonderful memories allows me to continue to honor him and the love we shared by moving forward. Desiring to love and be loved by another man does not mean I will ever forget Jim. In many ways, my heart is more open now than ever before. Loss will always be a part of our lives because of the growth, rebuilding, and transformation that has occurred since it.

"Hurry up and return to normal." What's normal? Grief is not an illness that lasts for 7-10 days, you take medication, and then you are back to normal. There is no time frame. Grieving people have changed—no, grieving people ARE changed. There has been restoration and rebuilding. We've grown, learned hard life lessons. We cannot be the same person after the loss as we were before the loss. Grief affects so many parts of our lives, emotionally, physically, spiritually, financially, behaviorally, cognitively. A loved one dying, on a very small scale, is metaphorically comparable to the little pebble that hits your windshield, causing cracks to continuously grow until the entire windshield needs repaired. The windshield through which we see the world has drastically changed. Our perspective has changed. Perspective is courageously permissive. Quit expecting us to return to the normal humdrum of a mediocre life of complacency, stagnancy, settling, and wishy-washy intentions. Life is deeper. Our ideas of happiness and success have changed. Daily decisions take on more meaning and purpose. We are more in tune, intense, determined, focused. Once you know the vulnerability of life, you appreciate the complexity of a life well-lived. We are not jealous, envious people. We don't want what you have. We grieve what we lost. Grieving people don't always know how to communicate what they want or what they need. Sometimes we don't even know. Be patient with us, just be with us, let us know we are not alone, ask questions, love us where we are. We don't expect or want you to do it for us, we just want you to be alongside us. Friends, put yourselves out there for us, so we can put ourselves out there for you.

Heavenly Father,

Only you see each moment of our days. Open our hearts to trust you. Guide our lives and help us to do your will as we move forward. Mend our areas of brokenness. We all make mistakes—restore us. Help us to keep our eyes on you and our feet planted on your firm foundation. We know we grow weary when we rely on ourselves, give us your strength and wisdom to rebuild our lives. We thank you for your love, goodness, mercy, and grace.

In Jesus name I pray,

Amen

Chapter 9 Questions for reflection:

1. Can you identify ways people have tried to make you fit into a box you are trying to break out of?

2. Are you someone that puts other people into boxes?

3. How do you define normal?

4. What struggles have you "grown through" versus "gone through?"

5. Read Isaiah 43:19

CHAPTER TEN

KEEPING an EYE on LIFE

"The real voyage of discovery consists not in seeking new lands but seeing with new eyes."
– Marcel Proust

In June 2017, I was celebrating the end of another successful school year and beginning to enjoy my summer. During a routine eye exam, I found out I had a partially detached retina in my left eye. Within a few days, my family and I traveled to an eye specialist who had also performed surgery on my right eye retinal detachment in 2004. He confirmed what my eye doctor said, and we looked at courses for treatment. I was given three options to move forward with my retinal detachment. The best option to preserve vision and limit re-occurrence was surgery. I was in shock, disappointed, and scared, but this surgery happened four days later. I knew this surgery simply had to be done. I would do my best to grow through whatever each moment brought. I would rely on others. My past experience with great doctors had taught me to trust what they said and to be obedient to their directions. I knew from experience this would not be pleasant, but I've been through worse. I knew God would heal me and take care of me. But it was such an unwanted, inconvenient, challenging knock to life as it currently was.

Surgery went as the doctor planned. The doctor performed laser surgery to repair the part of my retina that was torn and inserted a gas bubble into my eye to hold the retina in place as it healed. It was a challenging time physically for me. I had to lay on my right side for days, I wasn't allowed to exercise or do heavy lifting, and I had to position myself in a certain way. My eye hurt, and my pupil was dilated, which made my eye very sensitive to light. I experienced daily headaches. I couldn't drive for a period of time so I felt trapped in my home with one working eye. That was certainly not how I wanted to spend my summer days. However, I was very thankful for my family, the many friends, and neighbors that came to my house, brought food, picked me up to get me out of the house. Most of all, I was very thankful for all the prayers.

When I was told of my eye surgery, I immediately got a run-down of restrictions for *at least* eight weeks. While being told these restrictions, I experienced anxiety, disappointment, a gut-wrenching feeling that I couldn't shake, a familiar fear that I couldn't name. I'm a firm believer in experiencing things fully to move forward courageously, and I was soon to name that all too familiar fear. It was a fear of things being taken away from me. A fear of loss. Writing those words make my stomach turn, my eyes fill with tears, my heart ache, and my throat hurt from swallowing too hard. This detached retina was no comparison to the loss of my Jim (whom I longed for even more than I thought possible during that time), nor any comparison to the physical injuries, pain, and healing sustained from our auto accident. NOT EVEN CLOSE. But for me, the eye surgeons list of restrictions took away a lot. It took away seeing normally, a beach trip, smaller trips, serving at church, exercise, driving…summer…life as normal…life as planned…the list could go on.

I guess those things may seem small to some, but when that too-close-to-home fear was poked, the devil whispered in my ear. He whispered that my life would always be loss; that the rug would always be pulled out from under my feet. I listened. I grew discouraged. I grew quiet. It was hard. I lost sleep to worry and fear. There were many days that I gave my fear and anxiety to God in the morning only to take both back throughout the day. Then, I felt shame for not trusting enough, for not remembering all the lessons I learned though the accident, for missing all the joys of the day, for not having any control over anything. I beat myself up so much. Some days grew long and mundane, some nights were longer.

The days turned to weeks and weeks turned to months. It was now August, and normally that is a time to celebrate being refreshed and renewed from enjoying summer. Normally it was a time to get excited about going back to school. I still could not see well out of my left eye, my pupil was still dilated, I still had restrictions that limited me, I was still sometimes fearful, and I didn't have my summer. As a teacher, we treasure our summers! Even while I quietly battled, I had been having better days, going to the pool, driving, enjoying family and friends, and walking for exercise. I even found it exciting, if not a little overwhelming, to be starting a different teaching position.

Three days before Open House at my school, and almost eight weeks after surgery, I went to my eye doctor appointment for the fifth time. My parents drove me and we spent the entire day together. I sat in the lobby and began to pray for all the patients in the office. I prayed for the doctors, I prayed for personal healing and restoration. I got a good report. My eye was healed. My restrictions were lifted. The doctor told me that my gas bubble should be completely dissolved within a week to ten days, and that two weeks after that I could put a contact in that eye. I was immediately teary-eyed, shook the doctor's hand to thank him, hugged the nurse, and told God how great He was.

Three months after surgery, I went to my family eye doctor and was fitted for a contact in my left eye. The contact did improve the vision in my left eye. Being able to see a little better helped to relieve the daily nausea and headaches. But it was discovered that cataract had developed and I would need surgery. A lot of emotions came back to my mind while being told that I would need another surgery on my eye. I realized that there are always triggers that take us back for a brief moment to something else we've experienced. I had similar feelings of self-pity, questions of why, growing uncertainty of what would come next, and having to grow through something I just didn't want to do. But I'm convinced that God always arms us for what's to come. Unlike battles of war, battles of life are never won once! I continued to thank God for His healing, for the way He loves me, for his faithfulness and provision.

God continuously takes us through places where our relationship with him is strengthened and deepened.

Although I could not exercise physically throughout the months of healing, I did exercise spiritually and emotionally. There are three choices when going through trauma; we fight, flight (escape), or freeze where we are. Perseverance proves which one comes out on top. Sometimes you have to sacrifice your present comfort and convenience for a better future. The devil wants us off track, distant, feeling and acting like a different person than we really are. He convinces us that despair is the right medication for discouragement. Each day the devil's whispers can be silenced. God does not work through shame. God really wants to take away all our fear and anxiety. God's provision will fill us with more than we've lost. In having to keep distance from some things in my life during that time, I discovered what I wanted to draw nearer to. God knows us, sees us, fights for us, loves us, has a plan for us, and is good.

Heavenly Father,

Let us thank you for healing, even if it doesn't come as quickly as we want or the way we want it. Thank you for the health we have today. Each day, may we give you our fear and anxiety, and trust you with the outcome. We love you and our daily relationship with you.

In Jesus name I pray,

Amen.

Chapter 10 Questions for Reflection:

1. What are some things that cause you to lose sleep?

2. As you look back in your life, where do you see that God has strengthened and deepened your relationship with Him?

EPILOGUE

"God says don't worry about your future.
He is the author of your story and He's already
written the final chapter."
– Max Lucado

Writing this book has challenged and, ultimately, grown me. From the earliest stages of
dreaming of writing a book, to the actual writing of it,
God and I have pulled ghastly amounts of all-nighter
conversations. Writing was also very hard for me. I had
a lot to learn about the process and, emotionally, some
chapters took a lot longer as the majority of my time was

spent wiping tears off the keyboard. The point is, you have to fight harder to dream bigger to do bigger.

I'm finding these paradoxes of grief, healing, and rebuilding to be true. A death can awaken us to live our lives better. Suffering a loss can create a series of unexpected gain. When I lost myself, I had to find my new self again. When I lost my life with Jim, I had to find my new, yet very different life on my own. God is a God of multiplication and gain in Him. Turmoil around us can create peace in us. It's not that I found peace myself, but I found the One that is peace. Loneliness can show us Who surrounds us. In the stormy ocean of lies, there's always an Anchor of truth.

I've decided that I don't want to be conditional -- my days, my joy, my character depending on the circumstances around me. But that struggle is real and it's fought every day. I am trying very hard to apply the lessons I've learned to the life I now live. I know the only thing I really have any control over is me. I don't want to give life's obstacles any more power than they already have. My greatest fear is unfulfilled potential. A double-edged sword for sure, it can be my greatest driver and motivator, or it can also be one of the biggest obstacles—me, getting in my own way. I know I can only carry so much weight on this journey. I am working hard, with God at the wheel, to get rid of the excess weight. The excess weight for me is people pleasing, unforgiving, insecurity, pride, anger, shame, fear, control, worry. I'm confident my list could go on. My greatest weapon is still gratitude in the present moment.

One of the biggest lessons I've learned is that there comes a time when you have to surrender the life you thought you would have in order to fully embrace the life you could have now. I'm to this point in my life and it's really exciting, contagious, uncertain, and even a little scary at times. The flame inside me is burning stronger than ever. True, I may not have what I once thought I would, but I do have more than what I once thought I could. You will never hear me say that I'm thankful the accident happened or that I like it, but I will sing all day about the good God has done since it. And God hasn't just done great things in the past; He continues to do great things. He wants to meet us in the present moment, to give us new victories in Him. It's taken every second of the past six years to feel as blessed as I do today—to focus on what I've gained instead of just focusing on what I've lost. I need to continue to grow and learn, but I can say I am better than I used to be. God is continuing to grow and use me where I am.

We all know certain prayers all too well—the ones we pray each day, but nothing changes. That desire of the heart. That stirring that won't stop. Questions we want answered. Situations we want changed. Actions that need taken. As I learn every time I go fishing, I'm not the most patient person. If you put the words, "wait patiently" together, I am often not doing either. The devil can creep up in our times of waiting causing discontentment, selfish control, manipulation, the nudge to settle. Sometimes I trick myself by saying that now that I'm healed and ready that whatever I'm waiting for should immediately happen. These are the times that I need to rest in God's love and wisdom. Be obedient where I am. The good news is that God has been faithful and will continue to be so. He wants to reward our returned faithfulness. Trust that all is well in God's timing. Sometimes we try our hardest to muddy up the waters of our lives. But if we would just let the mud settle a bit, quit walking and just wait, some things would begin to clear. I pray often, and I want every bit of everything He has in store for me. Micah 7:7 says, "But as for me, I will look to the Lord; I will wait for the God of my salvation; my God will hear me."

Oddly enough, I was recently challenged by a trusted friend to write what I hoped the people in my life who know me best and love me most would say about me after I went to heaven. A possibly morbid thought, but I get the goal of this assignment. If I can put into words what I would want people to really feel and say when I'm gone, then now I can take the actions to live that life while I'm here. That's a gutsy reality check. I would challenge you, the person reading this book, to do the same. Here is what I hope people say about me: Kendra's struggle was a gift to grow her relationship with Christ. She loved. She served. She was authentic and intentional. Instilling hope in others, she enjoyed the journey and worked hard. Ephesians 2:10 says, "For we are God's masterpiece. He has created us anew in Christ Jesus, so we can do the good things he planned for us long ago." People saw Jesus working in and through her.

Questions for reflection:

1. What are some of your life's obstacles?

2. Where did you picture your life to be at this point? How have you embraced where God has taken you?

3. What do you want people to say at your funeral?

In closing, please allow me to pray for us one final time.

> *Heavenly Father,*
>
> *Only you see each moment of our days. Open our hearts to trust you. Guide our lives and help us to do your will as we move forward. Mend our areas of brokenness. We all make mistakes—restore us. Help us to keep our eyes on you and our feet planted on your firm foundation. We know we grow weary when we rely on ourselves, give us your strength and wisdom to rebuild our lives. We thank you for your love, goodness, mercy, and grace.*
>
> *In Jesus name I pray,*
>
> *Amen*

APPENDIX A

Max Lucado, *Every Day Deserves A Chance: Wake Up to the Gift of 24 Little Hours* (Nashville, TN: Integrity Publishers, 2007)

Max Lucado, *It's Not About Me* (Nashville, TN: Thomas Nelson, Inc., 2004)

Beth Moore, *Get Out Of That Pit: Straight Talk about God's Deliverance* (Nashville, TN: Integrity Publishers, a division of Thomas Nelson, Inc., 2007)

Joel Osteen, *It's Your Time* (New York, NY: Free Press, a division of Simon & Schuster, Inc., 2009)

Student's Life Application Study Bible (Carol Stream, IL: Tyndale House Publishers, Inc., 1992, 1994, 1997, 2004)

ABOUT the AUTHOR

Kendra Shea Wriston is a teacher, writer, and speaker. She coached middle-school basketball and assistant varsity volleyball for eight years, and has continued to teach in the same school district for seventeen years. Kendra is a life-long learner, and passionate about all things Jesus. Kendra is a dedicated daughter, sister, friend. Wriston lives in Canton, Ohio where she is involved in her church, community, leads an active lifestyle, and enjoys spending time with family and friends.

Follow me on Facebook
Tragically Transformed:
How God Turned Struggle to Gift

Follow me on Instagram:
@kswtragicallytransformed